The Reading Group

A Play

Fay Weldon

A SAMUEL FRENCH ACTING EDITION

SAMUEL FRENCH

FOUNDED 1830

SAMUELFRENCH-LONDON.CO.UK
SAMUELFRENCH.COM

FOR AMATEUR PRODUCTION ENQUIRIES

UNITED KINGDOM AND WORLD
EXCLUDING NORTH AMERICA
plays@SamuelFrench-London.co.uk
020 7255 4302/01

Each title is subject to availability from Samuel French,

depending upon country of performance.

CHARACTERS

Oriole
Tom
Lesley
Avril
Anne
Zelda
Harry

All are in middle age or later, except for Tom, who is in his thirties

The action of the play takes place in the front parlour of a house in a seaside town

Time: the present

INTRODUCTION

I received a letter from the Townswomen's Guild of a small town in Wales asking me if I happened to have by me a one-act play for five or six women which they could enter for a drama award. Most of those available, they complained, were out of date or old favourites and they wanted something new, which addressed the life of women today. I did not, of course, have anything by me answering their brief, but I didn't see why I couldn't provide one. I was deep into a long novel at the time and dearly wanted to take time off. So I put the novel to one side and wrote *The Reading Group*—where one or two or more women gather together in a room, my thesis was, home truths emerge ... especially if those women are not friends to begin with but are brought together by a common interest. In this case an enthusiasm for novels.

I was talking about the project to an actress friend—OK, I know the proper phrase is actor, but in this case the fact that she was female is relevant—and she said "but you have to have at least a couple of men in the play, so everyone can go down the pub after rehearsals". So I added two men. And I wrote it, loving every minute of it. I sent it off to Wales, thinking the group would be pleased. World Premiere and all that.

They weren't at all pleased. They were polite but definite. No, thank you. They wanted five women. Hadn't they said they didn't want men? And it was ten minutes too long. I wrote and said actually you *could* do it as an all-women piece, if you wanted. A simple matter of writing the Tom and Harry parts off stage, as it were. All Oriole has to do is describe her relationship with Tom when she and Lesley first meet, and insert a guilty phone call or two from the Tom in the pub, whence he has retreated, having delivered his ultimatum, before the action begins. We can do without the fun of meeting Tom in the flesh if we have to. Harry doesn't *have* to turn up at the end at all: he's been on the phone all the way through: let him continue the way he began. And thus we'd solve the time problem, too. No good. Thank you for your concern, wrote the Townswomen, but they'd already chosen another play.

So here it is, published in the form I originally wrote it, but the all-female re-write remains an option available to anyone who wants to undertake it. If members of the cast have novels they want to talk about rather than the ones I have—*Vanity Fair, Madame Bovary, Jane Eyre*—they should feel free to interweave them, so long as it doesn't jar with their stage personas.

And have a good time rehearsing and performing, and as the old theatrical saying has it "may your scenery never wobble"! (Whether there is any such saying I have no idea, but if there isn't, there should be).

Fay Weldon

THE READING GROUP

The modest but charming front parlour of a house in a seaside town: not much money, but lots of imagination: books, prints, crystals, mystic wall-hangings. Six non-matching chairs arranged in a circle, waiting to be occupied

To the left, a short corridor to the front door. To the back, a door to the kitchen. A phone in the corridor, another off the set, R

Oriole, astrologer, kittenish, fiftyish, charming, rearranges the chairs to best effect. Tom, her boyfriend, thirtyish, vaguely Eastern European, follows after her, protesting

Tom You're ashamed of me.

Oriole I am not.

Tom I can speak. I can think. I can read. I may be foreign but I have feelings. If you prick me do I not bleed, et cetera? I am not a log of wood, Oriole: I am a person. I am not too young or too male to suffer, to hurt, to be humiliated.

Oriole Darling, do stop. If there are five women and one man it won't work.

Tom Why not?

Oriole Because we will nearly be able to relax but not quite. If there were four women and two men, it would be fine but it would be another kind of evening. Or three men and three women. But five women and one man, no. I'm sorry, but no. There'd be all the disadvantages and none of the advantages.

Tom You mean my male presence would distract you. You would all compete for my attention?

Oriole Don't be absurd.

Tom Then why do you throw me out in this barbarous way?

Oriole I do not throw you out. I am simply asking you to go down to the pub for the evening. You live here in this house. You share my bed. You are twenty years younger than me. People have got accustomed to that; you're part of the scenery of this town. Fine. But if you insist on coming to a famously all-female reading group they will think you have strange powers over me and won't like it.

Tom I think it is very strange to have a woman-only reading group.

Oriole Oh, go and join the Taliban. Take it up with them. Novel reading is a female preoccupation, everyone knows.

Tom How sad. Here is a group of women who would rather read novels than live real life.

Oriole We would prefer to do both. But this is a small town, and sometimes there isn't enough real life to go round.

Tom I hate the pub. I like female company. I could bring in the coffee and stay upstairs the rest of the time.

Oriole No. You'd only bang and crash about over our heads to remind us of your existence. Tom, what have you got to offer on the subject of the English novel? Face it. Nothing.

Tom Everything. I am properly educated, albeit on the banks of the Danube. I can quote from Shakespeare and Milton, and name the novels of Dickens and Hardy, as well as can the next foreigner.

Oriole Dead White Males. DWMs. Sorry. We prefer to study contemporary fiction, written for women, by women.

Tom But you told me you did *The Horse Whisperer*. That was written by a man.

Oriole You are so argumentative. That was a kind of indulgence. A weakness. Because of the film. Because of Robert Redford, if you must know.

Tom Why do you find Robert Redford so attractive?

Oriole Only in a dream world, darling, you are attractive in the flesh, please don't worry about it. I have to work out a seating plan. Could you write out little cards for me, please? As for dinner?

He does too, obedient as ever. She finds wine glasses, and polishes them

Only five of us. Avril, Anne, Zelda, as usual, and Lesley, our newcomer from the big city. That's quite exciting, except she's a divorcee and no-one is ever quite sure about the desirability of a new single female turning up. Not of course that we're in competition for men. It's just a leftover, I suppose, from the old attitudes. What do people called Lesley tend to be like, do you think?

Tom If they are girls, their parents wanted them to be boys. If they are boys, their parents wanted them to be girls. One last time, please may I join the group?

Oriole No. I won't allow it. She sounded OK on the phone. An artist, she said, but that can mean anything. Born in June. Gemini. OK so long as you're not married to them, then it's which twin are you kissing? I know you think astrology is rubbish. That's because you're a Sagittarian. But it's how I earn a living: it's that or the dole; you should pay my profession more respect. (*She drops a glass, breaking it. She searches and finds a dustpan*)

Tom I didn't say a word. Allow me this, allow me that. Oriole, you pay me no respect. You have to make a decent man of me, you have to marry me.

Oriole So you keep saying. No. We're fine as we are. Oh, think about it. You are younger than my oldest son. Think of the wedding. How embarrassing!

Tom I'm older than the youngest son. What more do you want?

Oriole Why do you want to marry me?

Tom Because I love you.

She decants broken glass safely into an empty cereal packet

Oriole Yes, yes, yes. So you keep saying. So easy. Love is all around. All you need is love. That was back in the sixties. Look at where it got us. You don't hear the word much any more, people are frightened of it: especially me. Avril referred to it last week as neurotic dependency. Why Anna Karenina killed herself. Why Lewinsky got herself into that mess.

Tom You will go on hearing the word from me, regardless. It has meaning for me.

Oriole I can see it is useful: a cloak to cover a multitude of deficiencies. You don't understand us jaded English folk.

Tom Oriole, I'm not putting up with this. Either this is my home or it isn't. We share a life formally, or we don't. We are not going on as we are.

Oriole But I want to. I like it as it is. What's wrong with it? I am stunningly happy.

Tom If you don't marry me, I am going to leave you.

She continues as if he hadn't said this

Oriole! Did you hear me? I am not playing games. I'm not going to hang around as your toyboy. It is humiliating.

Oriole Oh, that old thing. The toyboy obsession.

Tom To be thrown out as and when it suits you: one minute it's OK for me to exist in your life, the next it's not. You never turn me out of your bed, I notice.

Oriole I never want to. I remember now. Your Mars has just gone retrograde in Scorpio. You're bound to be aggressive and paranoic. You'll feel better next week when Venus zooms to the rescue.

Tom Oriole, I mean this. My situation in this house, in this town, is intolerable.

Oriole Oh, go and find someone else. Some twenty year-old. Beat up on someone your own age.

Tom You take great risks.

Oriole You bet I do.

Tom Where would you find someone else like me?

Oriole That's the point, I don't need anyone, like you or unlike you. You are an optional extra. This gives me infinite strength.

The doorbell rings

Tom Don't answer that.

Oriole Of course I'm going to answer that.

Tom Your reading group is more important to you than our future.

Oriole No. I just think your timing is despicable.

Tom If you answer that bell it's the end for us.

Oriole Good. Don't make too much noise overhead packing.

Tom Don't think I haven't anywhere to go.

Oriole I bet you have.

Tom Of course I haven't, Oriole. How could I? I love you. I love your eyes, and your hair, and the way you are, and even your terrible moods. I have given up my life and followed you to this town at the back of beyond. I have no job, no profession, only you, and loving you. And I am despised for it. You are cruel to me, Oriole. All I want is to be able to hold my head up when I go outside this door. But you prefer to make nothing of me, nothing. Your optional extra.

The bell rings again. She stands undecided

Oriole Go to the pub. Come back at closing time. We'll talk about it then.

Tom We will not talk about it: you will give me an answer, yes or no. Ask your women friends what you should do.

Oriole You push your luck. And we will be talking about literature, not life. Thank God.

The bell rings. She answers it

Lesley enters. She is a Gemini, that is to say, quick, tricky, emotional and arty

Lesley I thought perhaps I'd got the wrong house.

Oriole No. I was just held up by an argument. You know how it is.

Lesley Not any more, thank God. I am a divorced woman. My time and my emotion is my own.

Oriole Who did the divorcing, as a matter of interest? Him or you?

Lesley I do hope this is to be a reading group, not an encounter group. You described it to me as a rest from the self.

Oriole Don't worry about it, it'll be fine when I've calmed down a bit. I'm Oriole Starr, a Taurus; you're Lesley, a Gemini.

Lesley And this is your son?

Oriole No, this is Tom Kapinski, my boyfriend, who is just going down the pub.

Lesley As they do.

Tom pauses for an angry second, before leaving. What can he say?

Oriole follows after, suddenly worried

Oriole Darling? Be happy...

But it's too late; he's gone. At least he didn't take his suitcase. Matters are simply on hold

Lesley It's wonderful to be without all that. The domestic row. I so love the space in the head——

Oriole No children at home?

Lesley They opted to stay with their father, and his new partner. I love them dearly but let her put up with them. I left everything, you know. Just walked out. Put behind me the bourgeois life, the possessions, the routine: everything so polished and perfect. Flowers could not exist, they had to be arranged. It was destroying me. My soul was about to die. You know how desperate one can get? I've always wanted to paint—now at last I can be free to be creative.

Oriole With me it was music. Then I was widowed. Now I cast horoscopes to keep off the dole. Well, never mind. I'm sure it will turn out all right.

Lesley Freedom to get up when you want, go to bed when you want, eat in front of the TV, never again have to see the boring friends who hate you anyway—now it's new people to meet, new ideas to have, a new life to start. Do you think I protest too much?

Oriole Yes. But I do remember all that. Intolerable. He didn't want me going out to work. Not earning is being like a child forever. Having to ask, even though he loves you, and you love him. Which I did.

Lesley I expect it takes time to settle into it, that's all. Mostly, I like buying what I want at Marks & Spencer, not having anyone look at the prices when you get home and saying but we didn't really need that, why did you buy it?

Oriole I can remember that part of it too. I don't want it again. Men like to control you. You have to fight it.

Lesley Mark's been very generous. He didn't argue about alimony. He said if I wanted to pursue my art, if that was my life imperative, and I couldn't do it married, then OK, we would be divorced. Everyone must pursue their own destiny. For an accountant he was very understanding.

Oriole That must have hurt a bit.

Lesley Yes. I suppose one did expect more of a fuss. Am I early or are the others late?

Oriole The others are late. (*She hands Lesley a glass of wine*)

Lesley That's enough about me. Sorry. It's if you don't talk to anyone all day... I've been to one or two reading groups in the past, though Mark always hated me going. In fact we'd quarrel quite badly about it, but you're right, you have to stand up for yourself. What kind of books do you do?

Oriole Last year we covered Margaret Atwood's *Alias Grace*; Toni Morrison's *Paradise*, only none of us could really work out what was going on, and we're not all that stupid; *Captain Corelli's Mandolin* and *The Horse Whisperer*.

Lesley *The Horse Whisperer*?

Oriole Well, it sort of gets to you.

Lesley But not in an intellectual sort of way.

Oriole But the fact that it gets to you is interesting. And how. And why.

Lesley I suppose so. I'm sorry I said that about the young man being your son, when he was your boyfriend. How embarrassing.

Oriole People do it a lot. Sometimes on purpose.

Lesley I mean really, why not? Men go round with younger women. It's good to see the tables turned.

Oriole No. It's just good to have someone who loves you. (*She pauses*) Did I say that?

The doorbell rings

The Lights fade to darkness then after a pause come up again

Our five women are now seated in their semi-circle. Oriole and Lesley we already know. Anne is a dedicated executive wife, smart, face-lifted, and nervy. Zelda is an attractive, rather abrupt, frizzy-haired, feminist idealist. Avril is sweet, gentle, calm and mysterious

Zelda I brought along a *Sunday Times* list of great books of the century. I thought we could choose from that.

Anne Yes, I saw that list too, Zelda, but I hadn't heard of a single book on it. I want a novel that applies to me and the kind of life I lead.

Oriole The people who make up those lists are trying to make us all feel illiterate. And they're succeeding.

Zelda You did ask me to be leader of the group. Couldn't you at least be advised by me?

Anne Well, of course, yes. It's just best-sellers of the century might make a more appropriate list for the likes of us. We might find something, well, easier.

Avril Perhaps we should be thinking about using our own judgement, not relying on lists, and not talking ourselves down.

Oriole (*to Lesley*) Choosing the book's always the most difficult part: you see us in our true colours. Stubborn. We get better later. I hope the wine's OK.

It isn't. Lying murmurs of "Fine, fine". Oriole feels the need to apologise

I didn't go to Tesco's, as I usually do. This was a special offer at the newsagents. They promised it was OK. It's been a really thin week, star-chart-wise.

Zelda (*amiably*) How you can earn your living the way you do, Oriole, out of other people's gullibility...

Oriole And how you can talk, Zelda, teaching children books you hate, just because they're on the National Curriculum...

Zelda What book?

Oriole *Jane Eyre*. You hate it. You told me so.

Zelda It may be a hymn to female masochism, but it's part of our national heritage. It goes with the job. Sorry.

Oriole OK, but don't you have a go at me.

Silence. Then Zelda apologises

Zelda Just slipped out, Oriole. Sorry. It's my star sign. Scorpio. Can't help it. Always stinging my own tail.

Avril The stars do not dictate our destinies; only suggest them.

Lesley Is it always like this?

Anne No. We're just all a bit fractious today. Personally, I love *Jane Eyre*.

Zelda That figures.

Anne See what I mean? Seriously, couldn't we do it?

Chorus No. Boring. Did it at school. No classics, per-lease.

Anne Oh, well. It just helps if people say, "Oh yes, your reading group, what are you studying?", and you can say a book they've heard of. I don't like the contemporary and modern. I hate all that language.

Lesley It's what happens in the real world.

Anne Not in mine.

Zelda OK, Anne, no heroin chic and addicts' heads down lavatories.

Oriole Anne's a Libran. She likes everything cosy.

Zelda Please, Oriole—no more red rags to bulls. What's the matter with you today? Quarrelled with lover-boy?

Oriole Of course I haven't. Bloody sceptical Scorpio, you.

Avril It's good for the group to express hostility, but never to nurture it. I'm a stress counsellor, and specialise in group dynamics. I should know.

Zelda I'm not in the least hostile to Oriole, she's my friend. I never knew you were a stress counsellor, Avril.

Anne My husband goes to a stress counsellor. His firm sends him.

It really does work, he's been so much better since he started going.

Lesley Books, anyone, books?

Oriole Understand, Lesley, that my friend Zelda here thinks my partner Tom is a toyboy and I am totally depraved, a victim of my sexual appetites.

Zelda I just think it's bound to end in tears. You're too old. OK everyone, settle down, that's enough bonding and anti-bonding.

Anne Couldn't we do *Madame Bovary*?

Zelda But that's a classic. I thought they were too difficult for you.

Anne I saw it on TV. It looked simple enough to me. I ready liked it. She had the prettiest little jet bag, embroidered with sequins. I've been looking for one everywhere, but jet's right out of fashion. I might get one made up.

Avril Madame Bovary was a compulsive personality. Always difficult for the spouse. Spend, spend, spend.

Lesley I've never read it. What's it about?

Oriole Young French woman married to really boring older man; she has lovers and longs for the bright lights. Men drive her to misery, debt and death.

Lesley From the sound of it, it's the bourgeois lifestyle does it. I can sympathise.

Zelda And me. Trapped in a small town existence, doing the right thing, so the only way out is death.

Anne We are cheering ourselves up!

Lesley I suppose divorce is the modern equivalent of suicide. You go on living in this world, not the next, that's all. You get an extra stab at life here. But it could be heaven or it could be hell, how would you know in advance?

Avril I expect the writer was a man.

Zelda He was. Gustave Flaubert.

Avril Then I expect that was why he made her commit suicide. In real life she'd just enjoy herself with her lovers, or run off with one of them. The writer just had to punish her, for having a good time.

Anne She's only unfaithful because her husband neglects her.

Avril Do you identify then, Anne?

Anne I suppose I do spend a lot. I am extravagant. But then Harry
likes me to look nice, I have to hostess dinner parties and go on
spouse weekends with the firm and they all buy designer clothes,
what am I meant to do? And I suppose I do get kind of bored. Do
you know, last year Harry went to Hong Kong twice, Australia
once, Amsterdam sixteen times, mostly with overnight stays, and
to Ottawa four times. He works so hard and late. And now the
children are gone it can get a little quiet, and I have to admit I am
sometimes tempted, it's hard to think all that other life is over, in
fact, yes, I do identify with Madame Bovary—forget I said that,
expunge, expunge, delete, delete, rewind—it's all over now
anyway. Harry's being fattened up for the Board, this year he's
been home ever such a lot. I love him dearly.

Lesley For every man who has an affair, there's a woman out there
doing it too.

Anne Perhaps we'd better not do *Madame Bovary*.

The Lights fade to darkness, then come up again

Zelda How many votes for *Madame Bovary*?

Avril's hand goes up; everyone else's stays down

Well, she's out.

Oriole Good. All those lovers taking advantage of her.

Zelda You're in denial, Oriole. Blind and deaf to common sense.
Look at your own life.

Oriole Tom wants to marry me. Otherwise he says he'll leave.

Lesley Oh well. I suppose it is more interesting than novels. I think
I'm going to like living in this town. I met Oriole's young man.
I thought he was perfectly charming and so good-looking. What's
he doing in a place like this?

Zelda Nothing. That's the point. He lives off her.

Oriole He has a problem with his visa. He's a qualified doctor. But
he's Hungarian, so he has to re-train. Catch 22. Can't get the visa
unless you have the college place, can't get the college place
without the visa.

Anne I do think the traditional way is best. There's a wedding, she keeps house and looks after the children, he goes out and battles with the world. Then they grow old gracefully together and enjoy their retirement, and look back on their lives with satisfaction. Of course there are ups and downs, but you work them through. That's the way I see it.

Oriole I tried, and he died when he was forty-six. I am in leftover life now. Penalty time.

Lesley Of course, if you get married, your young man will get citizenship and be entitled to grants and all kinds of things, won't he?

Oriole Yes. That is something I daresay has crossed his mind, as it has mine. But it's not his prime motivation.

Avril There is nothing wrong with self-interest. Women always married for a roof over their heads, to find a father for their children. Now if women are earning and the roles reverse, they shouldn't complain.

Lesley There are certainly a lot of Eastern Europeans over here snapping up unmarried women just to get citizenship. After the wedding they're never seen again.

Zelda George Bernard Shaw said marriage for a woman was a meal ticket for life. He also said it was legitimised slavery. Always contradicting himself, like all the best people. We could do a play, not a novel. Shaw's all text and introductions anyway.

Oriole What, *Back to Methuselah*? No thanks. For your information, Tom does not want to marry me for my nationality. He does not plan to leave me once he has it, he just wants to feel permanent and respectable and able to live in this town with some dignity, and have people saying "that's Oriole Starr's husband", not "that's Oriole Starr's toyboy".

Lesley So what's holding you up saying "yes"?

Oriole Thought of freedom lost, I suppose. Fear of commitment. Sheer terror, in fact...

Anne Why terror? What's the matter with marriage? Harry and I are really happy. I'd leap at the chance, if I were you.

Zelda Husbands must take up such a lot of time. I never tried marriage myself. I've been too busy earning my living. Better to burn than to marry, and there's always a passing lover if one cares to go down to the pub. I should be careful, Oriole, sending your Tom down for the evening. God knows what he'll pick up.

Lesley Marriage stops you being yourself. Of course you don't want to throw your brand new self away, Oriole. As soon as a man gets to be a husband, he starts telling you what to do.

Anne What do you say, Avril? Give us a clue, since you know so much. What would you do?

Avril One wonders about a young man who wants to marry a woman past child-bearing age. It strikes one as an immature neurotic dependency. What we used to call the Oedipus complex at work. Oriole is a mother figure. But my speciality is stress, not domestic relations.

Lesley Reading group? Forget it! Group therapy again.

Anne Harry goes to one-to-one stress counselling once a fortnight. He's been doing it for six months. He's so much happier as a result. He didn't even mind me coming out tonight.

Lesley One wonders why.

Anne No, one does not.

Lesley Perhaps he has plans to go out himself.

Anne Don't be silly. He's too tired. Once he's home he's always too tired to go out. And Viagra would simply kill him.

Avril In my experience, many executives, who quite frankly are often power freaks by instinct and training, suffer unnecessary stress consequent upon their failure to realize that conduct appropriate to the office is not necessarily appropriate to the home. I expect his counsellor has explained that if he trusts you with your freedom, he will feel more free himself.

Anne Well, yes, that's more or less what he told me. One up to stress counselling.

Lesley Is she pretty?

Anne Who?

Lesley The stress counsellor. Sounds pretty dangerous to me.

Anne It's a professional relationship. Don't be silly.

Lesley If I was a woman looking for a husband—and there are enough about, God knows why—first thing I'd do is train as a stress counsellor. You'd get an hour at a time of some high-powered executive's life, you'd encourage him to talk about himself, you'd be nice and sweet and attentive and concerned, all the things his wife will have stopped being years back—and if after a couple of sessions you didn't have him hopelessly in love with you, and preferring you to his wife, and wanting to seal the union sexually, you'd be kicking yourself. The stress counsellor—today's equivalent of Becky Sharp.

Avril We call it positive transference. A proper therapist knows how to handle it.

Anne That's just absurd. Harry goes to a man, anyway.

Lesley That's what he says. If it's a man it's probably worse. You wait for your Harry to come out as gay.

Oriole It's a horrible scenario, Lesley. Is that how your mind always works?

Lesley It never used to. I don't know what's the matter with me. I'm sorry. I'm upset. I try to see good in things and sometimes it all collapses and I can't.

Oriole But you wanted the divorce.

Lesley Yes and no. I found him in bed with my best friend. That wasn't why I left him, of course. It was only the trigger. You can't blame him. I refused to share his bed. I'd stopped fancying him. You have to be true to your own feelings, don't you? Don't you?

Oriole Oh God. I'm sorry.

Lesley I'm not defeated. I was planning to leave anyway. I came here and started a new life.

Avril There's no such thing. We take ourselves with us wherever we go, but if we take ourselves new, improved and feisty, that's good.

Lesley It was only sex. It shouldn't make a difference, but it does. And he was married to me. Married men are supposed to be faithful, come what may.

Zelda I don't know why women let themselves in for this kind of thing... If you try and share a life it always goes wrong. Look at us lot.

Oriole We're not a representative sample. We're the women who go to reading groups. We want to work things out. If we weren't neurotic we probably wouldn't.

Anne Most women live happily ever after.

Avril No. They tell themselves they do. Better no relationship at all than one which isn't working. Too many women make compromises.

Oriole That's a recipe for loneliness.

Avril Not loneliness. Aloneness.

Oriole Same thing.

Avril No. Aloneness is something good, to be aimed for.

Oriole Do you practice it? You never say a thing about yourself.

Avril Well, it is a reading group, not a group therapy.

Zelda So it is. In the nick of time, before this turns into total confessional. OK, if not *Madame Bovary*, what?

The Lights fade to darkness

Oriole I'm sorry the wine's so awful. It is, isn't it? I'll make coffee.

Anne Can I use the phone?

Oriole Of course. Use the extension in the hall.

The Lights go up on Anne, on the phone in the corridor. Another pool of light for Harry, the executive husband, comfortable with a whisky, off the set far right

Anne I just wondered how you were.

Harry I'm fine. Relaxing. Having a good time?

Anne It's very interesting over here.

Harry What book have you chosen?

Anne None yet. We nearly did *Madame Bovary* and then decided not to. Why are you being so nice to me these days?

Harry Aren't I usually?

Anne No. Once upon a time you'd say things like "you're neglecting your household duties", or "why can't you just read books, why do you have to talk about them", or "hens' tea party", and so on. Not any more.

Harry Did I? I'm sorry. That was the old unreconstructed me, gone for ever. Let's just say I know a little more about myself. If you want to feel free you have to allow others to be free.

Anne Is that what your stress counsellor says?

Harry I think I thought of it. No, perhaps the counsellor did first. It gets hard to tell who thinks which when you're in this kind of treatment.

Anne Every Thursday, isn't it? And these days you're always around on Thursdays. Never travelling. You must really value your sessions. I suppose you wouldn't describe yourself as a control freak?

Harry I have to be one at the office, but I see it isn't appropriate at home. Look, there's a programme on TV I want to watch. Shouldn't you be talking books? With your women friends? Why are you taking time out to chatter to me? Not that I don't appreciate it.

Anne It's a coffee break. You did tell me your stress counsellor was a man. Is that true?

Harry Of course it's true. What's with the paranoia all of a sudden? Why on earth should I lie? They say it's difficult for one partner to be in therapy and the other not. A lot of resistance does go on. Perhaps we ought to be organising treatment for you too?

Anne You've really got the jargon, haven't you, Harry?

Harry I don't think this conversation is going anywhere, Anne. This isn't like you. I do believe you're trying to pick a quarrel. I'm sorry, I prefer the TV. (*He puts the phone down*)

The Lights go up. The others are seated; Anne joins them

Zelda If we're not ruling out plays and we're fed up with the contemporary, we could always do *A Doll's House*. Ibsen. Pretty little Nora decides her life as a married woman in a small town in Norway is stultifying. She's treated as a child and so behaves like a child. She makes her break for freedom and leaves home. But perhaps it's too feminist a work for some of you to put up with.

Anne She left her children. It's hard to sympathise.

Lesley I left my children. They're better off with their father. They don't need me any more. Actually, they haven't taken any notice of me for years. The girl's seventeen and into raves and body-piercing, and God knows what at weekends, and Stephen who's fifteen has a closer relationship with his computer than he does with me.

Anne That's just adolescence. It passes. Nora's children in *A Doll's House* were only weenies. Unforgivable.

Lesley So what's a good age to do it at?

Anne There isn't one. Children can be grown up and married, and have their own families, but if their parents divorce it's the ground shifting under their feet. I've seen it happen. I'd rather die than it happened to mine.

Avril Children are more resilient than people think. They recover from parental breakup quickly enough.

Anne You just want to believe that. It isn't true. I don't want to do a play. Plays are all argument, and different points of view. I like an author telling me what's what. I did see *A Doll's House*, as it happens, and I think she was completely out of her mind to walk out of a good home like that. It opens with her coming in with Christmas presents. She can afford to shop: he makes a bit of a fuss about what she spends, but not nearly so much as Harry makes. She has maids to look after the children and a cook, and a husband who adores her, and she shouldn't have lied about getting money for his operation. Wives should be open with their husbands. (*To Avril*) Isn't that so?

Avril Of course. And husbands with wives. It's surprising how many lie within marriage. I try to teach my clients the importance of truth. I think it's often mere cowardice stands in the way of a full and frank assessment of where the marriage stands. The weakness is the desire not to hurt the spouse, and so the lie drifts on, and the bad marriage with it. The search should be for the authenticity of the self, which may indeed entail the end of the marriage, but so be it.

Lesley I don't see any virtue in seeing things you don't want to see. Picture me, back home early from the cinema to find Mark had already gone to bed, me opening the door to the bedroom, surprise, surprise. Oh yes, surprise all right. I could have done without seeing that. And then everyone tells you you must stick up for your rights and throw him out, even your best friend, so that's what you do, but because the kids want to stay with him, the bloody judge gives him the house, and here I am, living on my own in a small town at a reading group, living on almost nothing, lonely as hell so I end up telling everyone everything I'd rather they didn't know. I'm just a failure at life. I can't really paint, I've got everything set up at last, but all I do is stare at my easel. I thought it was my life's meaning, and I threw everything away because of it, but all it is is a hobby. Perhaps we could do Van Gogh's letters. That tells us what talent really feels like, and I just don't have it. Not the real thing. I got an A for Art at A Level, but my daughter got an A star, and she doesn't even take any notice.

Zelda Standards are lowered, don't worry about it.

Avril Lesley did the right thing. She didn't put up with second best. As for you, Oriole, don't trap yourself in a marriage to a younger man without money. You'll merely burden yourself with another child. Is that what you want?

Oriole I like children. And he doesn't want any of his own.

Avril So he says. Until he meets a younger woman who does. Then he will be off seeking his own advantage, and why should he not? Owning half your house, no doubt, and claiming half your income, like as not.

Anne All you think about is advantage, and money, and property. It's horrible. There is such a thing as love. When is she going to get another chance like this? They don't come along all that often.

Avril That's a strange way to see it. Any man is better than none!

Anne Yes well, you and I seem to have different opinions on everything. Perhaps you're a little bit stressed yourself. And guilty.

Avril Guilt is a pointless emotion. I don't feel it. I train others out of it.

Anne I bet you do.

Lesley Can we get on? Can we abandon the personal? Forget the dramas? Bloody men. I've read a very interesting contemporary novel, Maggie Gee's *The Ice People*. It's set a few decades in the future. There's apartheid between the sexes. Women are in power. The boy babies get fed oestrogen. Only problem is, there's an Ice Age coming...

The Lights fade to darkness, then come up on Anne, on the phone again, with Harry

Anne Harry, what is the name of your male stress counsellor?

Harry I don't know. I can't remember. Just some very neutral person in a room. Doctor something or other.

Anne Is there something you're not telling me?

Harry Of course not. I tell you everything. Truth's important in a marriage.

Anne Yes. So I hear. We all have to seek authenticity of feeling.

Harry I think so. Yes.

Anne And you're not likely to find that at home, are you, after thirty years of marriage?

Harry Has it really been thirty? Good God. What's the matter with you? What are you women doing round there? Sounds more like a conspiracy to me, this reading group of yours. What are they? Feminists, man-haters, marriage-breakers? You're a married woman, Anne.

Anne That sounds more like the old you. That's almost reassuring. I'll tell you what we are, we're women doing what we can to like men. It's difficult.

Harry Not all women hate men. I know quite a few who don't.

Anne Bet you do. Stress counsellors included.

Harry What has got into you? You say yourself how much better I've been since I started treatment.

Anne Oh yes. Singing in the bath, putting on your best tie on Thursdays. Do you think I'm a total fool, Harry?

Harry I'm certainly not. If I put on a dreary tie on Thursdays it's likely to get commented on. Stress counselling does not take place in a vacuum: all reports get read: personality gets assessed:

why would the firm pay for me to do it otherwise? I may make the Board, I may not.

Anne You've got an answer for everything, but you don't fool me. They're going to make you a director. You're going to be promoted out of my reach. I'm not going to be good enough for you any more. Not smart enough, or young enough, or pretty enough. I'm only a housewife. I'm boring. You're planning to leave me, you're seeking authenticity. That's what all this is about.

Harry Good God, Anne. You sound really upset. I'm coming round now to take you away. Before you start saying things that can't be unsaid.

Anne Oh yes, why don't you? You'll be in for a real surprise. (*She slams the phone down and goes back to the group and takes her place, the spotlight following her*)

The Lights come up

Zelda Everything all right?

Anne Yes, just fine.

Avril We decided not to do *Vanity Fair*.

Anne That's a pity. That schemer. Becky Sharp. She knew how to get what she wanted. We might have enjoyed that.

Avril I was quite for it. We might have found a good role model in Becky.

Anne What, self-interest at the expense of morality? Clawing your way to the top not caring who gets hurt? Becky sleeping with Amelia's husband? You think that kind of thing's an object lesson?

Avril I see no point in masochism. Want needs to come before ought.

Lesley That's certainly the way my ex-best friend felt.

Oriole I've never read *Vanity Fair*.

Lesley Battle of Waterloo time. Thackeray. There's good, trusting Amelia, who gives up everything for love of George, bad social-climbing Becky, who loves no-one and ends up powerful and rich. I did it at school. Can't we find a book in which the good get rewarded, and the bad get punished?

Zelda Doesn't even happen in the Bible.

Oriole If you're really good you get crucified.

Lesley I don't understand why we all keep trying to be good, that being the case.

Avril Exactly. It's the social gene. Altruism. To help others is to help ourselves. It's an instinctive response, not a rational one. If we resist we feel guilty. But we don't live primitive lives. We live in a complex society. The altruistic gene just gets us into trouble. We must resist its impulses when we can.

Anne That is the ultimate cynicism.

Lesley What's the best thing you've ever done, Oriole?

Oriole Mostly people ask what you've done wrong, not what you've done right. What I do right is a day to day thing: I don't just invent the daily horoscopes in the local newspaper: I study the stars and write up what they foretell. It would save me four hours' work a day just to cheat and make it all up. Lots do. I don't.

Zelda But astrology is nonsense anyway.

Oriole You may think so, sometimes even I think so, but within my own terms of reference I'm truthful. It's nothing dramatic, it's nothing spectacular. And I try to be honest in my relationships, and I try to trust and it's difficult. And I look at my face in the mirror and I see I'm falling to bits. My face sags, my eyes droop, my hair's gone wiry, I'm an old hag, I'm Madame Bovary twenty years on, Becky Sharp thirty. Why should I trust this young man to mean it when he says he loves me, or to mean it for more than the next weeks? Better get him out of my life now, before it hurts too much later.

All stare at her. They would like to give her reassurance but they can't

Lesley Zelda, your good deed?

Zelda My whole life. When I was twenty my mother had a stroke. I looked after her night and day for ten years. I missed out on what you could call the peak partnering years. When she died I made a virtue of necessity; now I enjoy the single life, and speak fervently in its favour. That seems to me the positive thing to do.

Lesley What's yours, Anne?

Anne I gave up my life for my family. I'm a wife and a mother, not an individual. People speak slightingly of me. "Just a housewife", I say. I have become a subsidiary person. All I have is moral power.

Oriole You look better than the rest of us. What is your good deed, Avril?

Avril Truth time. OK. None. I don't aspire to being good. I am the woman in Lesley's scenario. I have got to a certain age and I am tired of supporting myself. I don't have Zelda's patience. I don't have Lesley's capacity for self-deception, or Oriole's for attracting men. I am a dull person in myself, I know that. I am tired of getting up in the morning and going to an office, and putting a little away for my old age and never enough, so I have decided to get married. And being a rational person, I decided to go where I'd encounter the rich, competent and available men. Those on the promotional ladder, seldom at home, and subject to stress. It's going well. I have three powerful executives to choose from. All in love with me.

All stare at her, disconcerted

Zelda Why waste your time at a reading group?

Avril Men like well-informed women. Ask Anne. Why do you think she's here?

Oriole Not even a flicker of real interest, real enthusiasm, real enjoyment?

Avril Sorry. No.

Anne I'm surprised she said sorry. It isn't in her nature.

Avril A slip-up.

Anne She likes to get a closer look at the wives. She can play her cards better. She can assure the husband there was nothing worth losing. She knows, and she is believed. She has the arcane knowledge. Worse, it's her pleasure. Later she can think of the wife squirming. She likes that.

A ring on the doorbell

That will be my husband, Avril. Your Thursday afternoon client. We need this confrontation, I think. An end to wilful blindness. The lancing of a boil. I have you rumbled.

Avril has the grace to look startled, but quickly recovers

Avril Harry? We're to meet Harry? Well, that's fine by me. For once, Anne, you revealed just a little more truth than was wise. I've been waiting for it: women can't resist boasting. Harry has always suspected: now I can confirm it for him. Mrs Executive, with the Madame Bovary syndrome.

Anne I was making it up.

Avril What, an idle boast? Who's going to believe that? No, you've blown it, sister.

The doorbell goes again

Oriole This is unbelievable. I'll tell him everyone's gone home, shall I?

Anne No. Ask him in. Why not?

Oriole goes to answer the door

Lesley Actually, everyone, I think I'm going. Quite enough reading group for today. Back to the easel and sanity.

Zelda Me too. Back to the marking. I'm behind as it is. We can walk down the front together, Lesley. The street lighting's so bad. Even I get nervous.

Lesley Friends are the most important thing. I seem to be finding them at last.

Zelda You think you're the only one out of step, but everyone is much the same. No-one's life is in the least straightforward. This truth is both reassuring and appalling. All we can do for these people is not witness what happens next.

Lesley You're right. It's better as narrative.

Zelda and Lesley leave, brushing past Oriole and Harry, who remonstrate with one another in the corridor, leaving Avril and Anne to confront each other

Anne How dare you? How dare you come here and show your face to me.

Avril You with your face-lifts and your moaning and your spend, spend, spend. Harry likes a simple woman, sweet and gentle and non-demanding. Most men do.

Anne I bet you flatter him no end. Bet that's how you do it.

Avril Well, of course. Men only want what women want. Admiration and adoration. Naturally, I trowel it on. Your Harry is no different from any other man of his age and his kind. Gullible.

Anne You're not even younger than me.

Avril Older men don't need young flesh the way they did, or else they've given up trying to find it. Now young flesh can earn, it has got much more particular. And old flesh, of whatever gender, picks and chooses amongst the young. Look at Oriole, poor fool.

Anne You are unscrupulous, and the truths you tell are so unkind. He would see through you straight away. You're so nasty.

Harry and Oriole stand by the door. They've been listening. Avril has the grace to look perturbed

Harry Avril, what are you doing here?

Avril It's a reading group. That's all. I'm entitled. One can't be on duty all the time, surely. And you'd gone home to your wife. Only of course she didn't stay home, but went gadding as per usual. For once she actually came here, instead of using it for cover. Which I can assure you is what usually happens.

Harry You had no business. It will be the worse for you. I will not have you interfering in my wife's life.

Avril I'm sorry, Harry. I try to be tough and defiant but it doesn't work. It doesn't ring true, does it? It isn't really me. I only wanted to know what she looked like. I love you so much; even to be near her is to be near you. And that's the truth of it. Don't be angry with me. I don't mean any harm. I know you love me too.

Harry Don't you Lewinsky me. Love! You wouldn't know it if it hit you. You are a speculative bitch, tough as old nails, in the business of entrapment. Blackmail the Personnel Department as you like, threaten us all with sexual harassment, we will meet you in the courts. Anne, this woman is half-mad at the best of times, believes every man she meets is in love with her, and is a disgrace to her profession.

Anne You never tell me anything. Now see what's happened. She's right, there has to be truth in marriage.

Harry I went to Avril for exactly two most alarming sessions; the third I taped, I then reported her. We now employ a man, a Dr Leibowitz, or some such name.

Avril It was wrongful dismissal. I'll sue all right. I'll get compensation, in buckets. The way he looked at me: that was sexual harassment all right. You wait and see—I'll have your stupid face plastered over every tabloid in the country. See how you like that. You stupid, blundering, insensitive bully of an old man. As for you, you smug face-lifted cow, he's all you can get! You're a real Madame Bovary all right: her lovers all walked out on her, same as yours did, you seem to have forgotten that. Bloody reading group. Can't even decide on a book to read, forget that for a game of bleeding soldiers.

Avril exits, slamming doors. Anne, Harry and Oriole stare after her. Tom comes in as Avril leaves

Oriole Tom. It's you. Surely the pub isn't closed yet. But we're finishing early. It's OK. Come on in.

Tom No, it isn't OK. I've been listening to the men down the pub: they tell me all women are the same: they've turned into vipers. There is no way in the world you would marry me for love alone.

This is the age of self-interest. I'm outnumbered. In Rome do as the Romans do. I'll pack. Get the early train. I'll be out of your life and you can be happy.

Oriole If they're in the pub they're not going to like women very much. They're not a random sample, Tom.

Tom I am a stranger in this land. I won't embarrass you in front of your friends. (*He moves to go upstairs*)

Oriole stops him

Oriole Anne, Harry, Tom and I are going to get married. We're going to be man and wife. We're going to join the ranks of the old-fashioned and respectable.

Tom I don't believe it. What did they say? What happened? Why?

Oriole Because someone asks why, doesn't mean there's an available because. Becauses happen in fiction, I daresay that's why we get obsessed with novels. I dunno why. The triumph of hope over experience? You are the nicest man I ever met? You don't play games? You speak the truth? I don't want to lose you? You think of a reason, it'll do. Let's just say when I saw you again, I wanted to.

Tom I want more. And I want it said publicly, before these witnesses.

Oriole You are so foreign! OK. I love you.

Tom OK. How was the evening?

Oriole Oh, you know, as these things go. The men turn up anyway, we might as well let them in. A mixed reading group. People will get used to it. They get used to anything. I don't know why I made such a fuss.

Anne Can Harry come along too, then?

Harry Oh, good God! Are you out of your mind, woman?

Oriole winces. What has she done?

CURTAIN

FURNITURE AND PROPERTY LIST

Further dressing may be added at the director's discretion

On stage: Books
Prints
Crystals
Mystic wall-hangings
6 non-matching chairs
2 phones
Wine glasses
Bottle of wine
Tea towel
Dustpan
Empty cereal packet

Off stage: Glass of whisky (**Harry**)

LIGHTING PLOT

Property fittings required: nil
1 interior. The same throughout

Cue 1	Doorbell rings *Fade lights to darkness, pause, bring them up*	(Page 8)
Cue 2	**Anne:** "…better not do *Madame Bovary*." *Fade lights to darkness and up again*	(Page 11)
Cue 3	**Zelda:** "OK, if not *Madame Bovary*, what?" *Fade lights to darkness*	(Page 15)
Cue 4	**Oriole**: "Use the extension in the hall." *Bring up spotlights on* **Anne** *and* **Harry**	(Page 15)
Cue 5	**Harry** puts the phone down *Cross-fade to general lighting*	(Page 16)
Cue 6	**Lesley:** "…there's an Ice Age coming…" *Fade lights to darkness, then bring up lights on* **Anne** *and* **Harry**	(Page 19)
Cue 7	**Anne** moves back to the group *Follow* **Anne** *with spotlight then bring up general lighting*	(Page 20)

EFFECTS PLOT

Lightning Source UK Ltd.
Milton Keynes UK
UKHW02f1440220818
327639UK00006B/316/P